·PARRAGON·

HERBS
AND THE
KITCHEN GARDEN

KIM HURST

Illustrations by
BRENDA STEPHENSON

This edition first published in 1997 by
Parragon
Units 13–17 Avonbridge Trading Estate
Atlantic Road, Avonmouth
Bristol BS11 9QD

Produced by
Robert Ditchfield Publishers

ISBN 0 75252 141 1

A copy of the British Library Cataloguing in Publication
Data is available from the Library.

Typeset by Action Typesetting Ltd, Gloucester
Colour origination by Colour Quest Graphic Services Ltd,
London E9
Printed and bound in Italy

"With thanks to **J**"

SYMBOLS

Where measurements are given, the first is the plant's height
followed by its spread.
The following symbols are also used in this book:
 ○ = thrives best or only in full sun
 ◑ = thrives best or only in part-shade
 ● = succeeds in full shade
 E = evergreen
Where no sun symbol and no reference to sun or shade is
made in the text, it can be assumed that the plant tolerates
sun or light shade.

POISONOUS PLANTS

Many plants are poisonous and it must be assumed that no
part of a plant should be eaten unless it is known that it is
edible. Although many herbs have a medicinal reputation, it
is advisable to consult your doctor before treating yourself.

CONTENTS

HERBS AND THE KITCHEN GARDEN

Even the smallest garden can include herbs. Many are ornamental, most are fragrant and almost all accommodating enough to be tucked into odd corners. In addition, the culinary herbs can turn even the simplest everyday meal into a treat. Add to this a few of your own home-grown vegetables, freshly picked from the garden, and you have the makings of a feast – which will also be a healthy one.

Quite apart from this, growing and eating food of your own is economical, gives much pleasure and a sense of satisfaction. It need not be ambitious. Indeed, it is better to be cautious and selective at first, growing only crops you think will thrive in your situation (a precaution that is worth taking to avoid mistakes and disappointments). Instead, it might be something as simple and easy as a bunch of radishes, but pulling that first fresh bunch on a sunny day, brushing away the soil, washing the handful of bright red roots and munching them with a salad can give pleasure that is out of proportion to the effort.

GROWING HEALTHY FOOD

Growing your own produce also means that you have a say in what goes into it. You can make the choice to raise your crops organically, using only good natural methods, knowing that what you are eating has been grown without a chemical in sight. This is purely an individual decision that everyone makes for him or herself but it must be said that raising your own herbs and vegetables is an

Opposite: An exuberant formal herb garden.

Variety of leaf is a very great asset in herb gardens.

excellent opportunity to produce healthy and nutritious food which is free of chemicals. All that is needed is a good humus-rich soil, water, sunshine and your time. If your earth is difficult, raised beds are a very good substitute as you can fill them with another type of soil or a good organic compost. If reclaiming an old overgrown garden, start with a small area which can be easily managed. Once it is under control, move on to the next patch, and in this way you won't get discouraged.

Many of the herbs and flowers mentioned in the book attract beneficial insects into the garden, which in turn helps control pests. If you create an area within your garden for these plants, or include them amongst your vegetables, then the garden will in time develop its own natural balance.

A charming winter wall hanging of sweet bay and *Iris foetidissima*.

PLEASURE OF THE HARVEST

Harvesting your crops of herbs, flowers and vegetables starts early in the spring reaching an ultimate crescendo in the autumn.

In the spring you can gather fresh chives, chervil and parsley for soups, omelettes and salads; sweet cicely leaves for removing the tartness from rhubarb; hop shoots to steam and add to salads and savoury flans (or pick them to be eaten on their own with butter, when they are called poor man's asparagus, though I personally regard them as food for the gods!). This is also the season to pick the fresh new leaves of good king henry which is rich in minerals and iron. Steamed with fresh nettle tops and added to a cheese flan, it is a spring tonic for all.

Quickly summer moves in with an abundance of

salad crops, decorative red lettuce, wild blue chicory, and blue borage self-seeded amongst the carrots and beetroot. Bees hum round the flat heads of the elegant dill, moving down to drink from the bright orange faces of the pot marigolds. All add to that heady summer feeling. One of my hardest jobs at this time of the year is to remove the perfect blooms of my roses, cornflowers and the like, but if I am to savour their delights in the winter they need to be collected at their best and dried quickly to preserve their beauty and scent for pot-pourri.

Lavender, southernwood, balm and sage are a few of the other herbs which are collected in summer for their aromatic properties. They should be hung in bunches and dried to be used throughout the winter.

In early autumn the harvest really gathers speed. Now it is a rush to complete all the tasks that need to be done: picking beans and peas, gathering onions and garlic, all the freezing, drying, bottling and making of chutneys, pickles and other preserves. This always turns into a race against time before the onset of the first frosts. Yet it is worth it to capture all your work and enjoy the flavours in the winter as you have through the other seasons.

As I collect my herbs and flowers through the seasons, in my mind I piece together some of the decorations I shall make for autumn and winter with the dried material. These include sachets, pillows, wreaths, wall-hangings and many more delights as shown in the chapter on decoration.

We have now come full circle to the time when, after a good wholesome meal made with the fruits of your labour and maybe some home-made strawberry wine, you can sit down with some seed catalogues by the fire. At this point it is tempting to excite the imagination with wonderful names of plants from exotic places, and to dream up elaborate schemes and dishes with all the herbs, vegetables and fruits. But be warned that these do not always work and, for my part, past disappointments have

A small and beautifully designed herb garden showing how important is attention to details like paving and seating.

taught me better. I would suggest that you choose wisely, grow for your needs and pick varieties that are not so readily available in the shops. This is now my motto and it works. Knowing this, you can plan next year's crops with the insight that nothing can be more satisfying than growing your own.

1. HERB AND KITCHEN GARDENS

TRADITIONAL KITCHEN GARDENS

TRADITIONAL KITCHEN GARDENS were born out of necessity for the production and rotation of crops to feed the family for a year.

This modern kitchen garden has been subdivided to make access easy. This system will also make rotation easier.

◆ *The strong lines of this garden mean that it looks handsome even with areas of bare earth.*

The same garden two months later. Cropping has begun and flowers for cutting are in full bloom.

◆ *Note the long flowering season of the chives in the foreground.*

POTAGERS

A POTAGER, although often associated with the gardens of large country houses, is easily adapted to the small garden. Vegetables, herbs and flowers are planted as a design to give colour and form.

Good pathways are essential for easy tending and harvesting. Gravel, brick or bark are good mediums.

◆ *The paths of a potager both organize it and create a pleasing design.*

Beds in a potager can be edged by the path or by a small hedge – here, box surrounds this lavender bed.

◆ *Chives, feverfew or decorative cabbages would make a softer planted edge.*

A SMALL HERB GARDEN

HERB GARDENS do not require a huge area. Just a few plants of thyme, mint, parsley and sage make a valuable contribution to the kitchen but take up very little space.

1. You can make a herb garden in a very small area and still grow a useful number of plants. Most herbs prefer an open sunny position, but will tolerate some shade. Ensure the ground is well prepared and all weeds removed.

2. Subdivide the area to make access easy. The garden will also be more appealing if you can partition it off or give it some shape through either hard materials or patterned planting. Here a simple brick path has been laid to a hard area in the corner and tiles mark the near edge.

The designer of this small walled garden has taken great trouble over laying the paths and placed a seat where one can enjoy the scents of the plants in such an enclosed area to the full.

Charming small herb beds surrounding two cherry trees as part of a larger garden.

◆ *Hard surfaces help 'stabilize' the floppy nature of some herbs.*

EDGES *and* HEDGES

TRADITIONALLY herb and kitchen gardens had some sort of formal hedging and this was both a practical and decorative means of shaping the garden.

Dwarf box hedges interweaving to form the intricate pattern of a knot garden, creating spaces for planting herbs or siting pots.

◆ *Such a knot will take about three years to establish, but needs regular clipping.*

Box (*Buxus sempervirens*) Hardy evergreen shrub. 'Suffruticosa' is a dwarf form. Take cuttings in spring or autumn. E

Hyssop (*Hyssopus officinalis*) Hardy evergreen shrub. Blue, pink or white-flowered forms. Trim in spring to keep its shape. E

Lavender (*Lavandula*) In small gardens try a compact variety like *L. angustifolia* 'Hidcote' or 'Munstead'. E

Hedge germander (*Teucrium chamaedrys*) Bright pink flowers midsummer. Ideal knot garden plant. E

Feverfew (*Tanacetum parthenium*) Gives a softer edge. Easy to grow with appealing white daisy flowers.

Chives (*Allium schoenoprasum*) Useful edging and companion plant to keep away pests. Divide every second year.

CARPETING HERBS

HERBS THAT CAN CREATE a carpeting
effect offer the bonus of suppressing
weeds as well as giving off aroma.
Planted along edges of pathways they
creep along naturally, softening the
overall look.

***Thymus serpyllum* 'Snowdrift'** The thymes are ideal
spreading shrubs for covering sunny areas in gravel
gardens, patios, rock gardens or anywhere you need a
fragrant evergreen mat.

◆ *Propagate by taking softwood cuttings in summer.*

Corsican mint (*Mentha requienii*) For small areas, a creeper with a peppermint scent. Tiny leaves and purple flowers. Semi-E

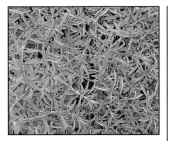

Creeping savory (*Satureja spicigera*) Ground hugging, highly aromatic. Needs a well drained, sunny position. White flowers. E

Creeping pennyroyal (*Mentha pulegium*) Bright green foliage and mauve flowers, said to keep ants at bay. Prefers moist soil.

Lawn chamomile (*Chamaemelum nobile* 'Treneague') Bright green, apple-scented foliage, non-flowering. E

This urn is surrounded by a dense planting of chamomile at the centre of a formal herb garden.

POTTED HERB GARDENS

HERBS ARE SUCH GOOD SUBJECTS for pots. Most enjoy the restriction and well-drained medium that can be provided in a pot.

PLANTING UP A POT

Use good nutrient-rich compost, preferably organic peat-free, and add to this a handful each of grit and coarse sand for drainage. Fill half of the pot with compost, then start to plant from the centre outwards.

Suitable plants would be one well shaped rosemary, surrounded by parsley, chives, oregano, winter savory, sage and French tarragon, interspersed with three trailing nasturtiums for colour and use in salads.

Standard bay tree Of all the herbs, a potted standard bay tree is the most prized. Snipping leaves off for culinary use helps to keep the shape, if you use your eye correctly. Re-pot and dress every year. Feed regularly. E

One great advantage of a potted herb garden is that you don't have to cultivate areas of land. Replacing a plant is very simple.

◆ *Invasive herbs like mint, bergamot, oregano and lemon balm can be contained to prevent them smothering other plants.*

POTTED KITCHEN GARDENS

SMALL-SCALE KITCHEN GARDENS can be very productive in containers, such as old sinks, wooden boxes, troughs, buckets, enamel bread bins and hanging baskets. Salads, courgettes, dwarf beans, salad herbs and cascading tiny tomatoes, if fed and watered well, will give a good crop.

Old wheelbarrows are very popular containers for ornamental plants, but can just as easily be made into small kitchen gardens.

◆ *Ensure that contained plants are watered regularly and that they have an adequate supply of fertilizer.*

Tomatoes are probably more often grown in pots than in the open ground. They need warmth and sunshine for fruits to develop and ripen.

Green peppers (capsicums) are also particularly suited to pot culture. Pots can be moved to take advantage of sunny positions and the plants fed and tended more easily.

Runner beans growing up a central support. If raised in the warm in the spring, the plants will crop earlier than outdoor sowings.

Even if you have just a small concrete yard, you can still grow fresh peas.

2. THE GROWING YEAR

PERENNIAL HERBS

EARLY SPRING sees the first green shoots of the sweet cicely pushing through, to begin another year's cycle. Other perennial herbs have had to contend with winter weather above ground – rosemary, sage, thyme, all evergreens. Chives, mint and marjoram appear gingerly until a brief warm spell spurs them into earnest growth with the rest of the perennials following.

Handsome clumps of blue-flowered rosemary and purple-leaved sage add to the varied textures of this border.

◆ *A planting of perennial herbs like this requires minimal upkeep.*

YARROW
(*Achillea millefolium*)
Ancient wound and tonic
herb. Infuse flowers to
make a facial steambath.
Flowers dry well for winter
decoration.
○, up to 1 × 1m/3 × 3ft

CHIVES
(*Allium schoenoprasum*)
Used for many hundreds of
years for their delicate
onion flavour and abundant
production of leaves from
early spring to the
beginning of winter.
○, 23 × 15cm/9 × 6in

GARLIC CHIVES
(*Allium tuberosum*)
Well drained soil necessary.
Also known as Chinese
chives. Slower growing than
common chives with a
shorter season. Leaves long
and flat with a distinctive
garlic taste.
○, 30 × 20cm/1ft × 8in

ANGELICA
(*Angelica archangelica*)
Grow in deep moist soil.
Majestic short-lived
perennial. Young stalks can
be candied or added to
jams and jellies for a
different taste. 1.8 × 1m/
6 × 3ft

HORSERADISH
(*Armoracia rusticana*)
A rampant grower.
Documented for thousands
of years as a food
flavouring. The roots are
freshly grated for sauces.
Use sparingly.
60cm/2ft × indefinite
spread.

FRENCH TARRAGON
(*Artemisia dracunculus*)
Needs a warm sheltered
place, protection in winter
and good drainage. Grows
well in a cold greenhouse.
Good vinegar herb. O, up
to 1m × 60cm/3 × 2ft

COSTMARY
(*Balsamita major*, syn.
Tanacetum balsamita)
Known also as alecost, once
used to flavour ale. Monks
used a leaf in their bibles as
a bookmarker and insect
repellant.
1m × 60cm/3 × 2ft

FENNEL
(*Foeniculum vulgare*)
Grow in well drained loam.
Tall elegant plant. Mild
liquorice flavour. Use young
leaves and stalks for soups,
sauces, mixed salads and
with fish dishes.
2.2 × 1m/7 × 3ft

Sweet Woodruff
(*Galium odoratum* syn.
Asperula odorata)
A creeping woodland herb
used to enhance the taste of
white wine. Dried it smells
of new mown hay and is
good for pot-pourri and
herb pillows. 30cm/1ft

Curry Plant
(*Helichrysum angustifolium*)
Needs light soil. Attractive
silver foliage plant with
small yellow flowers.
Distinctive curry scent.
Good edging plant. Flowers
dried for pot-pourri.
◑, E, 60 × 60cm/2 × 2ft

Hop
(*Humulus lupulus*)
Hop flowers are used for
ale. Pick tender young
shoots in spring, steam and
serve with butter, like
asparagus. For humus-rich
soil. 7 × 2m/23 × 6ft

Hyssop
(*Hyssopus officinalis*)
Good hedging plant and
bee plant. Monks used it to
flavour wine and liqueurs.
Can be dried, and used in
pot-pourri.
◑, E, 60cm × 1m/2 × 3ft

BAY
(*Laurus nobilis*)
Often preferred as a standard bush. Dried leaves in casseroles, game dishes, paté, marinades, soups. Crumbled leaves in pot-pourri. Not fully hardy.
○, E, 7 × 1.5m/23 × 5ft

LAVENDER
(*Lavandula* spp.)
Aromatic foliage and flowers. Dry flowers when first out. Pot-pourri, scented sachets and perfume. (See also 'Edible Flowers').
○, E, up to 1 × 1m/3 × 3ft

LOVAGE
(*Levisticum officinale*)
Distinctive yeasty celery flavour. Leaves for soups, stews, casseroles, marinades. Use seeds for bread, to sprinkle on salads, or make a savoury tea.
2.1 × 1m/7 × 3ft

LEMON BALM
(*Melissa officinalis*)
Good bee plant. Musky lemon scent to leaves which taste good in salads, soups, herb bread, cakes and sauces. 60 × 60cm/2 × 2ft

APPLEMINT
(*Mentha suaveolens*)
Woolly textured leaves with
a delicate minty apple
scent. Use finely chopped
in salads and dressings.
◐, 1m × indefinite spread

GINGERMINT
(*Mentha × gentilis*)
Leaf-tips used to decorate
food. Tear small amounts of
leaves into a mixed salad,
dress with olive oil.
60cm/2ft × indefinite spread

PEPPERMINT
(*Mentha × piperita*)
Mainly used as a digestive
tea. Dried for herbal sachets
and pillows to ease colds
and blocked sinuses. Pot-
pourri.
45cm/1½ft × indefinite
spread

MOROCCAN MINT
(*Mentha spicata* 'Moroccan')
Sharp mint flavour makes
excellent mint sauce and
jelly. Shred a few leaves into
green salad and dress with
lemon juice. 45cm/
1½ft × indefinite spread

SPEARMINT
(*Mentha spicata*)
Often known as garden
mint. Mint sauce and jelly.
Add to cooked vegetables
and salads. Dries well. Use
dried flowering tops for
herbal decorations. 45cm/
1½ft × indefinite spread

PENNYROYAL
(*Mentha pulegium*)
Two types, upright and
creeping. Strong
peppermint scent. Good for
paved areas. Insect
repellant.
15 × 30cm/6in × 1ft

BERGAMOT
(*Monarda didyma*)
Tea herb. Dried whole plant
in pot-pourri. Fresh leaves
sparingly in salads and
dressings. Good bee and
butterfly plant. For well-
drained soil.
1m × 60cm/3 × 2ft

SWEET CICELY
(*Myrrhis odorata*)
First herb to appear in the
spring, last to die back in
the autumn. Leaves are
anise-flavoured. Cooked
with tart fruits reduces
acidity. 60 × 60cm/2 × 2ft

CATMINT
(*Nepeta cataria*)
True herbal catmint, not so
decorative as purple-
flowered *N. × faassenii*.
Unusual pungent scent
which encourages the
attention of cats, often to its
detriment.
60 × 45cm/2 × 1½ft

POT MARJORAM
(*Origanum onites*)
A good herb for seafood
soups, eggs, fish, meat,
poultry, game, stews,
vegetarian dishes, salads
and sauces.
60 × 60cm/2 × 2ft

OREGANO
(*Origanum vulgare*)
Use leaves for
Mediterranean dishes,
pizza, tomatoes, *bouquet
garni*, seafood casseroles
and roasting meats. Dry
flowering stalks for
decoration.
15 × 60cm/6in × 2ft

BISTORT
(*Persicaria bistorta*)
Once used as a wound herb.
Early spring use young
leaves in salads or steamed
as a vegetable.
1m × 60cm/3 × 2ft

COWSLIP
(*Primula veris*)
A favourite spring flower.
Flowers used in jam, wine
and pickled. Dried flowers
and powdered roots in pot-
pourri. 23 × 15cm/9 × 6in

ROSEMARY
(*Rosmarinus officinalis*)
Much loved for its cleansing
properties. Many varieties
including pink and white
flowered. Use sparingly for
roast meats, herb butters,
oils, vinegars.
○, E, 1 × 1m/3 × 3ft

SORREL
(*Rumex acetosa*)
Acidic plant to be grown in
quantity for use in sorrel
soup and sauce. Broad
leaves useful for wrapping
foods. 60 × 60cm/2 × 2ft

BUCKLER LEAF SORREL
(*Rumex scutatus*)
Smaller arrowhead leaves
have a sharp citrus tang.
Good for green salads,
vegetable soups, omelettes,
sauces for fish.
30 × 60cm/1 × 2ft

SALAD BURNET
(*Sanguisorba minor*)
Cucumber-flavoured leaves
which can be used in salads
and sauces. Iced fruit drinks
benefit from the cooling
taste of this herb.
30 × 30cm/1 × 1ft

GREEN SAGE
(*Salvia officinalis*)
Good bee plant. Use in
moderation for stuffings,
sausages, pork dishes, to
flavour cheese. Batter leaves
and fry.
◑, E, 60 × 60cm/2 × 2ft

WINTER SAVORY
(*Satureja montana*)
A few chopped leaves with
broad (fava) beans or a
bean casserole add a tangy
spicy flavour.
38 × 30cm/15in × 1ft

THYME
(*Thymus vulgaris*)
Many edible and decorative
varieties. The culinary
forms are used for stock,
marinades, oils, sauces and
soups.
◑, E, 30 × 30cm/1 × 1ft

DILL
(Anethum graveolens)
A tall elegant feathery
leaved annual with umbels
of tiny aromatic blooms.
Aniseed flavoured leaves are
used in salads and fish
dishes, and the flowers and
seeds for pickles.
60 × 15cm/2ft × 6in

CHERVIL
(Anthriscus cerefolium)
Use in soups, sauces, salads,
egg dishes and to decorate
food. An annual, left to its
own cycle it will self-sow.
25 × 25cm/10 × 10in

CELERY LEAF
(Apium graveolens)
Use this celery-flavoured
annual in soups, casseroles,
pickles, curries, salads and
sandwiches. Rich in
vitamins and minerals.
60cm/2ft

BORAGE
(Borago officinalis)
Superb bee plant. Self-
seeds. Bright blue star
flowers to decorate food
and drinks. Annual.
75 × 30cm/2½ × 1ft

CARAWAY
(*Carum carvi*)
Ancient findings of caraway
show it has been used for
centuries. Seeds sprinkled
over meats, goose, beef
stew, soups, breads, cakes.
Biennial. 60 × 30cm/2 × 1ft

WILD CHICORY
(*Cichorium intybus*)
Bi/perennial with beautiful
powder blue flowers which
attract bees and butterflies.
Root dug, cleaned, roasted
and then ground makes
chicory coffee.
1 × 1m/3 × 3ft

CORIANDER
(*Coriandrum sativum*)
This pungent herb has been
used medicinally, as an
aphrodisiac and by the
Chinese for immortality! We
use it now more for its
culinary virtues. Annual.
60 × 30cm/2 × 1ft

SWEET BASIL
(*Ocimum basilicum*)
Grow in a heated
glasshouse and only plant
out when weather is warm.
Protect from heavy rain,
bruises easily. Tender
annual. 45 × 30cm/1½ × 1ft

GREEK BUSH BASIL
(*Ocimum basilicum* var.
minimum 'Greek')
A good variety to grow in
pots on the window-sill,
with miniature highly
aromatic leaves.
20 × 20cm/10 × 10in

CURLED PARSLEY
(*Petroselinum crispum*)
Garnish herb. Raw in salads
and sandwiches, cooked in
egg dishes, soups and fish.
Breath freshener. Biennial.
30 × 15cm/1ft × 6in

FLAT LEAF PARSLEY
(*Petroselinum hortense*)
Has the same properties as
the curled but a larger plant
with a stronger flavour.
60 × 30cm/2 × 1ft

SUMMER SAVORY
(*Satureja hortensis*)
Stronger flavour than
winter savory. Delicate
pink/purple flowers attract
bees. Upright growth like a
small tree. Use as winter
variety, for bean and tomato
dishes especially. Pot-pourri.
30 × 30cm/1 × 1ft

THE VEGETABLE GARDEN *in* SPRING

SPRING IS A BUSY TIME in the vegetable garden. When the soil is sufficiently dry to be worked, it should be dug over and raked to a fine tilth. If you apply fertiliser, this should be done at least three weeks before sowing.

SPRING SCHEDULE

1. Sow under glass or in heat for early crops. Plant outside when worst of frosts are past.	Summer cabbage, cauliflower, celery, leeks, lettuce.
2. Sow under glass in heat and plant out only when all frosts are past.	Runner beans, courgettes (zucchini), maize, outdoor tomatoes.
3. Sow direct into the soil when it has become manageable and worst of frosts are past.	Broad (fava) beans, beetroot, broccoli, Brussels sprouts, cabbage (summer and winter), carrots, cauliflower, celery, kale, leeks, lettuce, onion sets, parsnips, peas, radishes, salad onions, spinach, turnips.
4. Sow direct into the soil when worst of frosts are past, but protect from frost by earthing up.	Potatoes.
5. Sow direct into the soil when all frosts are past.	French beans, runner beans, courgettes (zucchini), maize.

CROP ROTATION

If you grow the same crops in the same position year after year, you encourage a build-up of the pests that prey on the crops and deplete the soil of nutrients. A regular annual rotation will help overcome the problem. Here we show a simple three-year system. None of the crops within each group should be planted in the same position as any of the others in the group for at least three years.

Group 1 Peas, beans, onions, leeks, celery.

Group 2 Brassicas (cabbages, cauliflowers etc.), turnips.

Group 3 Mixed crops – carrots, parsnips, beetroot, courgettes (zucchini), potatoes.

Grow quick-growing crops like lettuces and radishes with any of the groups as space becomes available.

PEAS

Sow early to mid-spring, at intervals, in a flat-bottomed trench 15cm/6in wide and 5cm/2in deep, in 3 rows 5cm/2in apart. Support seedlings with twigs, adding netting or rows of string on upright stakes as plants grow taller.

Harvest early to midsummer, about 3 weeks after flowering.

BROAD (FAVA) BEANS

Sow late winter under glass, spring outdoors, 20cm/8in apart in double rows, with 60–90cm/2–3ft between. Sow 5–7.5cm/2–3in deep, with a dibber. Support with string tied to stakes at the corners of the row. Pinch out the top of the plant when in full flower, to discourage blackfly.

Harvest regularly from early summer, when beans are 20cm/8in long.

FRENCH BEANS

Sow indoors in early spring, outdoors in spring. Sow 5cm/2in deep, 7.5cm/3in apart in single rows 45cm/1½ft apart. Thin to 15cm/6in apart. Keep well watered at all times. Stake climbing varieties and pinch out the main tips when they reach the top of the canes.

Harvest midsummer onwards when beans are 10cm/4in long.

RUNNER BEANS

Sow from late spring onwards, 5cm/2in deep and 15cm/6in apart, in double rows 30cm/12in apart. Support plants with canes, one per plant, pushed into the soil at an angle and tied to its opposite cane a short way from the top. Pinch out the main tip when plants are 30cm/12in tall.

Harvest summer to early autumn, when beans are 15–20cm/6–8in long.

Onions

Most easily grown from sets, onions are planted in mid-spring 10cm/4in apart in rows 40cm/16in apart, so that the tip just shows above the soil.

Harvest in late summer when the leaves are brittle, dry in the sun and store in a cool airy place in wire bottom trays.

Salad Onions

These should be grown close together, in rich, fertile soil raked to a fine tilth.

Sow at intervals from late winter onwards, under glass until the danger of frost has passed. Sow thickly 1cm/½in deep, at 1cm/½in intervals, in rows 15cm/6in apart. Do not thin, but keep weed-free, taking care not to damage the leaves or bulbs.

Harvest as soon as the onions are big enough, and use fresh.

Celery (Self-Blanching)

Sow indoors in early spring. Do not cover the seeds, place in a plastic bag and keep moist at 13°C/55°F. Prick out 5cm/2in apart and keep warm. Harden off the plants and plant out in early summer, in a block, 15cm/6in apart. Fix black polythene round the edge of the block to aid blanching.

Harvest celery from midsummer as required, before frost.

Spinach

Sow in late winter under glass, spring outdoors, thinly in drills 2.5cm/1in deep and 30cm/12in apart. Thin to 15cm/6in apart. Keep well watered, especially in dry weather.

Harvest. Pick leaves off the plants as required, frequently to avoid bolting.

LEEKS

Leeks prefer soil of an open free-draining texture.

Sow seed from late winter onwards, under glass at first, thinly in shallow (5mm/¼in) drills 30cm/12in apart. Keep seedlings well weeded and thin to 15mm/¾in apart, then later to 15cm/6in apart. To get white stems, blanch them by gradually earthing up soil around the plants from early autumn.

Harvest from late autumn, as required, Leeks will tolerate frost and be edible until spring.

MAIZE (SWEET CORN)

This tender plant must have a sunny sheltered site.

Sow indoors in spring, outdoors in late spring, in twos, removing the weaker seedling. Harden off indoor plants and plant out in early summer 38cm/15in apart, in a block.

Harvest late summer, when the silks on the cobs are brown and pressing the kernels produces a milky liquid.

LETTUCE

Lettuce is available in many varieties, the cabbage or butterhead lettuce, the cos, the crisphead, and the loose leaf, cut-and-come-again varieties such as Salad Bowl and Lollo Rossa.

Sow every two weeks from mid-spring to late summer in drills 2cm/¾in deep and 30cm/12in apart. Thin to between 15cm/6in and 30cm/12in according to the size of the variety. Loose leaf lettuce is sown in a block and thinned to 5cm/2in between plants.

Harvest as soon as mature as lettuces easily 'bolt' – run to seed. With loose leaf lettuces, cut the leaves as required.

Lettuce is an ideal catch crop, that is, one which matures quickly and can be planted between rows of slower growing vegetables. Also good are radishes, salad onions and summer turnips.

Cabbage

Sow summer-autumn cabbages and savoys outdoors mid to late spring 20–30cm/8–12in apart. Water generously. Spring cabbages are sown in late summer, transplanted in autumn, and fertilized from late winter.

Harvest spring and summer-autumn cabbages when ready, and savoys from early autumn.

Brussels Sprouts

These will overwinter but must have a fertile soil.

Sow in a sheltered spot in early spring in drills 30cm/12in apart. Transplant when 15cm/6in high. Work in fertilizer and keep properly watered. Weed well and stake tall varieties.

Harvest from late autumn onwards, from the bottom upwards.

Broccoli

Rich, fertile well manured soil is essential.

Sow in spring both calabrese and purple sprouting in drills 1.25cm/ ½in deep and 38cm/15in apart. Thin seedlings to 15cm/6in apart. Keep plants well watered.

Harvest calabrese in summer, cutting the main head while the buds are still tight and leaving the stem to produce side-shoots. Purple sprouting will be ready from the following mid-winter.

Kale

Grow in a sheltered part of the garden.

Sow seeds in late spring, 2.5cm/1in apart, in drills 1cm/½in deep and 20cm/8in apart. Thin to 7.5cm/3in, then to 38cm/15in when plants are 15cm/6in high. Keep well watered.

Harvest in winter, cutting small young leaves from the plant's centre as required.

CAULIFLOWER
Soil should be open and fertile.
Sow indoors in mid-winter, at 13°C/55°F. Plant out in early or mid-spring. Keep weeds down and earth up stems to keep plants firm.
Harvest from early summer, as soon as they are ready.

CARROTS
Sow under cloches in early winter, and at intervals from late spring to summer, in drills 15cm/6in apart. Thin to 5cm/2in, then to 10cm/4in if larger carrots are required – best done in the evening to avoid carrot fly.
Harvest from early summer, according to variety, as required.

TURNIPS
Summer turnips must be grown rapidly and make good catch crops.
Sow outdoors in early spring, thinly in drills 1cm/½in deep and 23cm/9in apart. Thin to 7.5cm/3in, then to 15cm/6in.
Harvest summer turnips when they reach the size of a golf ball. Winter varieties will be ready in mid-autumn.

BEETROOT (GLOBE)
Sow seed clusters from mid-spring onwards 15mm/¾in deep, 12cm/5in apart in rows 30cm/12in apart. Thin to the strongest seedling. Water frequently in dry summers and weed carefully.
Harvest as required from summer onwards, when they reach the size of tennis balls.

POTATOES
Sow earlies in early spring, maincrop later, 38cm/15in apart in trenches 15cm/6in deep and 60cm/2ft apart, eyes upwards. When plants are 15cm/6in tall, draw up the soil between the rows to make ridges round them. Repeat every 3 weeks.
Harvest earlies from late summer, as required. For maincrop, remove the foliage when yellow, and lift 3 weeks later (autumn).

PARSNIPS
Sow outdoors in late winter/early spring, in drills 1cm/½in deep and 30cm/12in apart, with 3 seeds together at 15cm/6in intervals. Thin to the strongest seedling in each group.
Harvest from autumn onwards, as required, but before the ground freezes.

COURGETTES (ZUCCHINI)
Fertile, well-drained soil is essential.
Sow indoors in spring in pots, outdoors in very late spring, in twos, 2.5cm/1in deep and 10cm/4in apart. Remove the weaker seedling. Feed and water liberally.
Harvest as soon as they are large enough (10cm/4in), to encourage further fruits.

RADISHES
An excellent catch crop or for children to grow.
Sow outdoors, every two weeks, from spring onwards, thinly in drills 5mm/¼in deep and 15cm/6in apart. Thin to 5cm/2in apart. Do not allow the soil to dry out.
Harvest as soon as they are ready (3–4 weeks in summer).

Asparagus

Asparagus needs a well-drained rich soil in a warm, sheltered part of the garden. The previous autumn, dig in plenty of well rotted manure or compost.

Year 1 In spring dig trenches 25cm/10in deep, 30cm/12in wide, and 90cm/3ft apart. Start with one year old crowns from a reputable supplier and place them 45cm/18in apart in the trench, spreading out the roots. Cover with 7.5cm/3in of soil. Hoe the soil between the trenches regularly, each time drawing a little soil over the plants until the trench is filled. In autumn cut down the foliage and apply a mulch.

Year 2 Apply a general fertilizer in spring and cut and mulch again in autumn.

Year 3 You may now harvest, but only one or two spears from each plant, leaving the foliage to build up the plant's strength. The following years you may cut for a six week period from mid-spring.

Tomatoes

Tomatoes are usually grown under glass in temperate climates, but may be grown outside in a sunny, sheltered spot.

Sow seed indoors in early spring and keep at a temperature of 18°C/65°F. Prick seedlings into individual pots of loam potting compost when the first pair of leaves appear, then pot on as they grow until they are in a 25cm/10in container. Tomatoes may be put outside in early summer, after hardening off. Water the pots every day and give liquid tomato feed weekly. Pinch out any side shoots and pinch out the top when the plant has eight trusses. Support the stems with canes.

Harvest in summer. Pick the ripe tomatoes with the calyx on. Any tomatoes still green at the end of the summer may be ripened indoors.

SOFT FRUIT

THERE ARE FEW PLEASURES of the table
to equal sampling one's own home-
grown raspberries or redcurrants.

A summer feast of blackberries, raspberries, redcurrants,
strawberries and gooseberries. The growing of blackberries
has been revolutionized by the introduction of spineless
varieties to ease picking. 'Oregon Thornless' is a popular
example with handsome foliage. Raspberries too have been
improved with sweet-tasting autumn fruiting varieties that
are good when frozen. There are also long-established
yellow varieties of raspberries as well as the newer 'Fallgold'.

TREE FRUIT

THE INTRODUCTION of dwarfing and semi-dwarfing rootstocks has enabled gardeners to grow a wide range of fruit trees even in small gardens. Where space is very limited, it is possible also to grow fruit against walls, fences or on wires in the form of cordons, espaliers or fans. These need careful pruning. It is essential to remember that if you grow only one fruit tree, it must be a self-fertile variety, so always check with the nurseryman whether the variety you want needs another tree to pollinate it.

Plums need a sunny wall. Ensure you have suitable varieties for cross-pollination, though some varieties such as 'Victoria', are self-fertile.

Espaliered apple in blossom. The horizontal wires are about 2.5cm/1in from the wall to allow air to circulate.

Grapevines can be grown as cordons or espaliers and will need strict training or they will take up much space.

◆ *Check with the nurseryman that your choice will grow in your district.*

Pear grown as an espalier. Make sure that your varieties pollinate each other. Even 'Conference' which is often considered self-fertile will crop better with a partner.

3. DECORATIVE
VEGETABLES AND
SALAD HERBS

DECORATIVE PLANTS

MANY VEGETABLES AND SALAD CROPS are handsome enough to be almost designer items in the kitchen garden, or, equally, in herbaceous borders. Attractive leaves, stems, pods, or flowers qualify them for both. A careful choice of these varieties will ensure that the kitchen garden is full of colour. There are for example purple-podded peas, red and white runner (stick) beans, and red forms of cabbage, lettuce and Brussels sprouts. Add to these the dark opal basil (*Ocimum basilicum* 'Dark Opal') and the magnificent silver-leaved cardoons or globe artichokes, and the scene will rival the flower garden.

Courgettes (zucchini) are treated as potted foliage plants and placed either side of a fuchsia.

◆ *Pots are ideal for maintaining a succession in a narrow bed like this.*

An array of ornamental brassica in pink, red, purple or white. These make stunning container plants. They are not eaten.

◆ *They can be treated as hardy annuals.*

Climbing gourds are not edible but can be grown for decoration.

◆ *The ornate gourds can be harvested for use in the house.*

EDIBLE FLOWERS

THERE IS AN ANCIENT TRADITION of eating certain flowers or using them for colour, flavour and decoration in food.

A beautiful flower petal salad makes the centrepiece of any summer meal. This one contains the flowers of chives, marjoram, nasturtium, borage, pot marigold petals on a bed of gingermint leaves, red orach, buckler leaf sorrel, salad rocket and salad burnet leaves.

ROSE PETAL JAM

Add orange-juice and lemon juice (2 table-spoonfuls of each) to 150ml (¼ pint) of water and boil together with 500gm (1 lb) of white sugar to make a syrup. Chop finely the red rose petals which you have already gently washed and dried, and add to the mixture and simmer for about half an hour, stirring continuously. Pot into little sterilized jars and seal.

Roses The petals can be used in several ways as food, but take care to remove the bottom of the petal (where it joins the stalk) first. The petals can be crystallized to make a cake decoration, or cooked for rose petal jam.

The little blue flowers of borage, orange pot marigold, heartsease and nasturtiums can be combined with other ordinary salad ingredients of the kitchen garden.

Lavender The flowerheads can be added to vinegar or oil which they will flavour. Otherwise, they can be crystallized.

Courgette (Zucchini) A fashionable way of eating the large melon-orange flowers is to dip them in batter and fry them.

Heartsease (*Viola tricolor*) Once introduced, this is a permanent, charming member of the garden as it self-seeds. Use the flowers in salads.

◆ *When you use flowers as food, whether fresh or cooked, be sure that they have not been sprayed with chemicals.*

4. GATHERING
AND DRYING

DRIED FLOWERS

IT IS IMPORTANT TO CHOOSE the right moment to pick flowers for drying. To begin with, they must be in peak condition. There must be no trace of bruising which creates fungal problems, nor of mildew which will spread contamination. Choose a dry spell and gather them after the dew has left them, for dew-moisture will cause troubles from mould; yet you must also pick them before the mid-day sun which will rob them of their volatile oils.

Use scissors or secateurs so that you cut their stems cleanly and then place them in a large basket or box. Put them on a table and sort them into bunches, making sure you pull off any dead or pest-damaged leaves, but leave foliage which is in good condition on the plant. Keep your bunches of flowers thin because they will dry more quickly. Hang them up to dry, head down, in an airy place at a steady temperature. An airing cupboard may be suitable, but the place doesn't have to be dark, so long as it is out of direct sunlight.

A basket of fresh feverfew, oregano, yarrow and mint ready for drying.

Lady's mantle (*Alchemilla mollis*), monarda, rosemary, dill flowerheads and buddleja mint.

An enchanting barrow of dried flowers. Seed heads, teasels and flowering grasses are used both as fillers in arrangements and to give structure and shape.

◆ *The colours of dried flowers are so subtle that in combination they look like a tapestry.*

INDEX OF PLANTS